Enda Walsh

DISCO PIGS

and

SUCKING
DUBLIN

Two Plays

LONDON

NICK HERN BOOKS

To my parents. A special thank you to Pat Kiernan.

A Nick Hern Book

Disco Pigs and *Sucking Dublin* first published in Great Britain in 1997 as a paperback original by Nick Hern Books Limited, 14 Larden Road, London W3 7ST

Reprinted 1998

Disco Pigs and *Sucking Dublin* copyright © 1997 Enda Walsh

Enda Walsh has asserted his right to be identified as the author of this work

Front cover: Eileen Walsh as Runt and Cillian Murphy as Pig

Typeset in 10 on 12 point Times by Country Setting, Woodchurch, Kent, TN26 3TB

Printed and bound in Great Britain by Athenaeum Press Ltd, Gateshead, Tyne and Wear

ISBN 1 85459 398 6

A CIP catalogue record for this book is available from the British Library

E

En

th

wi   ᴘtation of

A   ᴡinter of 1994, *The Ginger Ale Boy*

in ᴛhe ꜱpring and Autumn of 1995, and *Disco Pigs*, which
played in Autumn 1996. *Sucking Dublin*, for the Abbey
Theatre's Outreach Department, was seen in Dublin in Autumn
1997. He is currently writing a one-man show, *Love Underneath*,
and developing *Disco Pigs* as a feature-length screenplay for
Temple Films.

Enda Walsh won the 1997 Stewart Parker Award for *Disco
Pigs* and the 1997 George Devine Award for *Disco Pigs* and
Sucking Dublin.

A Selection of Other Titles in this Series

DISCO PIGS

Characters

PIG

RUNT

Disco Pigs was first staged in September 1996 at the Triskel Arts Centre in Cork by the Corcadorca Theatre Company and subsequently at the 1996 Dublin Theatre Festival. It was given its UK premiere at the Traverse Theatre, Edinburgh on 7 August 1997. The cast was as follows:

PIG	Cillian Murphy
RUNT	Eileen Walsh

Directed by Pat Kiernan
Designed by Aedin Cosgrove
Sound Design by Cormac O'Connor

Disco Pigs was workshopped for a week prior to rehearsals.

Lights flick on. PIG *(male) and* RUNT *(female). They mimic the sound of an ambulance like a child would, 'bee baa bee baa bee baa!!'. They also mimic the sound a pregnant woman in labour makes. They say things like 'is all righ miss', 'ya doin fine, luv', 'dis da furs is it?', 'is a very fast bee baa, all righ. Have a class a water!' Sound of door slamming. Sound of heartbeats throughout.*

RUNT. Out of the way!! Jesus out of the way!

PIG. Scream da fat nurse wid da gloopy face!

RUNT. Da two mams squealin on da trollies dat go speedin down da ward. Oud da fookin way!

PIG. My mam she own a liddle ting, look, an dis da furs liddle baba! She heave an rip all insie!! Hol on mam!!

RUNT. My mam she hol in da pain! She noel her pain too well! She been ta hell an bac my mam!

PIG. Day trips an all!

RUNT. Da stupid cow!!

PIG. Holy Jesus help me!!

RUNT. Scream da Pig mam! Her face like a christmas pud all sweaty an steamy! Da two trollies like a big choo choo it clear all infron! Oudda da fookin way cant jaaaaa!!

PIG. Da two das dey run the fast race speedin behine!

RUNT. Holy Jesus keep her safe. Holy Jesus keep her safe!

PIG. Mamble my dad wid a liddle mammy tear in da eye! I'm da liddle baba cummin oud, dada, I'm yer liddle baba racer!!!

RUNT. Da trollie dey go on

PIG. an on

RUNT. an on

PIG. an on

RUNT. an on

PIG. an on

RUNT. an on

PIG. an on!

RUNT. My mam she suck in da pain, grobble it up an sweat it oud til da liddle skimpy nighty itgo,

PIG. black wet black.

RUNT. Two gold fishys oudda da bowl!!!

PIG. A gasp gaspin! I'm ja liddle baba commin out! Open up ja big fanny!

RUNT. Trollie stop!

PIG. An leg open!

RUNT. Da fatty nurse schlap on with the rubbery glubs! stop! An leg open! Da two fat sous pooshhh an pooosshh ta spit da babas oud!!

PIG. Push girls push!!

RUNT. Scream da das oudsize!

PIG. Scream da das oudsize!

RUNT. My da he wan fur his din dins real fas, yeah!

PIG. Take your time love!

RUNT. He say, stopwadch in han! Da fannys dey look like donna kebabs!

PIG. Bud looka da liddle baba heads!

RUNT. Pooosh da baba poosh da head!!PIG. Pooshh mam poosh!! Poosh da Pig

RUNT. An Poosh da Runt! She wan oud mama!

PIG. An he wan oud, ta dada!

RUNT. Pooosh sous pooosh!!

PIG. We da liddle born babas!

PIG & RUNT: Pooosshhhhhh!

Silence. We then hear the sounds of babies crying. Music.

RUNT. An it wuz.

PIG. Nineteen

RUNT. Seventy-nine.

PIG. An da liddle baby beebas a Pork Sity take da furs bread inta da whirl.

RUNT. Da hop-i-da-hill all Bambi an Thumper!

PIG. Hey looka da liddle bunny, baby!

RUNT. An looka da nursey face, is sall rosey like a buuk full a roses!

PIG. An da two liddle babas all wrappt in pooder, ka nice smell pooder!

RUNT. My mam's nighty pink!

PIG. An my mam's nighty pink!!

RUNT. An my mam she pain no more! Sorta happy wid wat she fart out.

PIG. Bud my mam she cry all blubbery wid dad sittin on da bed flickin thru da Echo!

RUNT. Yeah, Pork sity was luvly amay bak den.

RUNT. Da peeplah dey really nice. Dey say,

PIG. She's a lovely little thing!

RUNT. Goo ga goo!

PIG. Look the little button nose!

RUNT. Ahhh gaga ga!

PIG. And the fingernails, ahhh look!

RUNT. Goo gee gee!

PIG. She's happy in that pram.

RUNT. Gaa gee goo goo!

PIG. She looks just like her mam.

RUNT. Fuck off ja!

PIG. Nell may bak den an me an she weez take a furs bread inta da whirl. A bobbly baby-boots girl she

RUNT. Runt! An a fat fatty fatso fart by da name a

PIG. Pig! But fatty no more! As ja can say, Slimfast fans!

RUNT. Oud we bounce inta a whirl of grey happiness!

PIG. We wa beautiful amay bak den!

RUNT. *Jar* beautiful! *Jar* beautiful, Pig!

PIG. Beg yer pardon, pal! *Jar* beautiful! Jar beautiful! Da liddle baby babbies a Pork Sity!

RUNT. Sa tell em who was furs sa!

PIG. Runt a cause!

RUNT. Tell em who was secon sa, saucey!

PIG. The Pig!

RUNT. Owney one sec tween da girl an da boy! An us no brudder or sis or anyth!

PIG. Fuckin amaz-zing, man! (*Pause.*) Les go Marbyke, yeah!

RUNT. Righ so!

PIG. Race ya!

PIG *and* RUNT *run racing each other. Sounds of heavy breathing.* RUNT *stops and looks at* PIG *continue.*

RUNT. So off we go! Zoomin as always! Pig's a real fass! Down da Marbyke Bark we go war dem mens an womens do da race an all. I wadch da Pig race an he run really really fass aboud da trak, yeah. Sonia O' Sullivan tinks Pig migh be da superstar star!

PIG. Ya noel ol Sonja . . . dem light weight running vests aand panties mean no-ting when ya got the finish line in sites! Ya gotta believe girl . . . without that yer fuck all! (*To* RUNT.) Les go my place.

RUNT. Me da runnin don matter dat much! But see whadda Pig wear? I choose dem! Splendid! I one step ahead in dat race, race fans! Fashion my life. Was goin down downtown, righ in da bum hole a Pork Sity, sall import ta me, yeah! I noel betta den mos fox down French Crotch Street! Pig, he nee da big big elp, dat fella. Withoud Runt poor Pig look like da sausies withoud da skin. Crap!

PIG. Is a hippyidy happidy birrday for my pal Runt n' me!

RUNT. Happy birrday, to you.

PIG. Happy birrday to you, pal too! 17, hah?

RUNT. 17 yeah! Pig?

PIG. Yes oh ligh a my life, my liddle choccy dip!

RUNT. Wa colour's love, Pig?

PIG. Love? Don no! Wa sorra love, love?

RUNT. Don no!

PIG. Hoy Mam! Way da din dins! Way da sausies an da saucey, hey mam! Schlap it there la!!

PIG *and* RUNT *eat. We hear the sounds of them eating mixed with them oinking. They stop.*

RUNT: Las get righly gone, ya on! Cider back a da bed yeah?

PIG. Up up up up up up up up up up!

RUNT. Down da gob an grab da lot! Up for it are ya?

PIG. A hippidy happidy in it?

RUNT. Les go!

PIG. Race ya so!

RUNT. Ah fook yes!!

PIG and RUNT *drink. It is a race.* PIG *breaks off and goes to the toilet. Sound of pissing.*

PIG. Good, in't she? Gallon by gallon deep we go! A buddel a rider's an awful ting, yeah, but hey, an wad da fuck! Da ting it works! Inta da skull like ka lawn mower it mix me an Runt all aboud! Two fishys a swillin it back a swillin it back a swillin it back . . . down da belly an oud da spout! Ders me dad a decoraten per use-jew-al. Give it up will ya! get a job, ja langer!

RUNT. Hey, Pig man!

PIG. Hey luvvy! Dis roam is it all! Da ress a da house is par shitheads an wankers! Dis roam is my kingdom! Pig da king! My bed da trone . . . da clodes dat Runt did make . . . sacred! Me an Runt . . . brudder and sis bud much maw, drama fans! We jar it! We fuckin jar ya know! Excuse me but odders are weak, yeah . . . like spa children ja drown in da river, I drown my mam an dad *now*! If dad no so busy wid da wallpaper a cause! Da faggot, scone head!

RUNT. Ta da bum hole shall we go?

PIG. Shall we cause!

RUNT. Quids?

PIG. Pock-full a tens!

RUNT. Regal!

PIG. Les go so!

RUNT. Les go so disco!!

Loud disco/techno music follows. PIG *and* RUNT *scream and chant 'Seventeen'. Music eventually stops. Sound of bus stopping.* PIG *and* RUNT *get on the bus.*

PIG. Las time Pig an Runt eva give mona to da bus . . . mus a bin a baba, a lease! Why nee ta pass wid any kish? Bus boss he well loaded yeah! Jacussi in sall da bedroams, I bed. So me an Runt jus barrel on!

RUNT. Come here to me!!!!

PIG. Scream da ugly wase fat cunt of a diver!

RUNT. Fook off!

PIG. Say Runt. Problem solve yeah! Easy. He noel his place. Sits. Drive da bus on. Slow. I sees him liddle eyes in da mirror! He scare in da eyes! Pig raise da han . . . Bus fass now. Good.

RUNT. Bus stop . . . stop bus!

PIG (*recognises someone*). Oh yes. Yes.

RUNT *laughs*.

PIG. Foxy locksy, in it?

RUNT. Is Pig.

PIG (*stands*). A birrday giff! Cova me, girl!

RUNT. Will, Pig.

PIG. Righ so! Hi dee hi!

PIG *mimes kicking Foxy around the place.* RUNT *narrates.*

RUNT. Pig an Foxy go all da way! Pig hate Foxy! One nigh, yeah, Pig he gasp for da glug glug glug glug! Down ta Blackcruel we drool. Off licence war Foxy work. Did work mo like.

PIG. Free drink, pretty please.

RUNT. No ney panic button Foxy he panic. He say 'I can't Darren'. Pig he get da buzz in da ead he wanna fisty!

PIG. I ass ya nice, nice man! Han fuckin ova!

RUNT. 'You know I can't'.

PIG. I fuckin kill ya!

RUNT. 'Darren!'

PIG. I get ja mam fuckin burn her, boy!

RUNT. 'The boss will kill me, Darr . . . !'

PIG. A shut yer gob, shut yer gob, shut yer gob ya fuckidy-fuck!

PIG mouths RUNT's lines below.

RUNT. Took Pig ten mins smash all buddels in dat drink shap. All but one yeah. Pig take da buddel Bacardi slinky . . . he kiss da buddel . . . an off. 'Pig! Jar pock-full a tens!' He stamp na Foxy face. Da nose like tomato itgo squish n' drip drop. Foxy cried, cried like his mam jus bin smack in da ead by da golf club . . . which she war . . . nex day.

PIG. Shmackkk!!!

RUNT. Pig hate da Foxy. He hate em.

PIG. Schmack schmack schmack schmack schmack schmack schmack schmack schmack schmack schmack!! An let dat be a less on ya Foxy! Dis bus is no purr you!!!

Sounds of a quiet bar. Television can be heard. RUNT and PIG look around. RUNT whistles God Save The Queen. PIG laughs.

PIG. Pig n' Runt stop tear furs. Is a sleepy ol' provo pub ta Pork purr years, yeah! Runt always do dat. Funny ho hey?! (*He laughs.*) No soul drink ere! No one gis a fuck aboud dem nordy bas-turds. Way bodder? News a da week is let dem do each odder in!

RUNT. Use-jew-al?

PIG. Oh yes darling. (*RUNT gets drinks in.*) I park a top a da seat by da pool an jus calm an wadch! Good like! Don cost no-ting eeder! I tink bout Foxy an my boot ta jaw face. I let da buzz go bye bye an down my ead it go . . . Pig breed it oud. Calm brudder calm down. I wadch in real calm now. (*Pause.*) Is a sad ol place dis! De ol town, yeah! Nine peep-lah inall, cludin dat bar keep. Big dime steamer him. Marky. Marky. ' Hoy Marky! dat a Tang Top?!' (*He laughs. RUNT returns.*) Ta ta, girl. Some ol man, alco mos likely, he sit at da bar lashin inta da spirit. He talk bouts Jack Charleton an a liddle tear come to his eye when he says . . . Dinny Irwin . . . Roy Keane! A fling a beer mat dat go Schmack! Roy Keane, I know dat fella . . . oh yeah . . . madge him cry an cry . . . an him ol-ler an all!

RUNT. Rea, Pig?

PIG. Oh yes. Roy a da Pullovers I used call him!

RUNT. Nancy was he?

PIG. Was ta me, girl!

RUNT. Wow!

PIG (*they toast*). To you, pal.

RUNT. To you, Pig. (*Pause.*) Got a gawk at dat postur, Pig!
En ter tain ment!

PIG. Tom Borrow evey, ol pal!

RUNT. Sad sad story! Boo hoo whoo!!!

PIG. Boo hoo whoo!

RUNT. Boo hoo whoo!!

PIG. Boo hoo whoo!!

They laugh. Big silence.

PIG. Da delly playin a show wid Terry Wogan. He watch dees
tings dat go all da wonky yeah. He's Irish, Terry Wogan.
Really funny! Real good show, delly fans! Top show!

PIG *looks at the telly and goes into fits of laughter.* RUNT
laughs too.

PIG. Les go disco! Les go wild one!!!!

PIG *and* RUNT *in a nightclub. They dance. They are well
gone. The music is loud.*

PIG. Jus me jus me jus me jus me jus me!! Oh yes!! Dis da
one!! Real soun set Pig swimmin an swimmin in da on-off
off-beat dat is dance! Beat beat beat beat beat thru da veins
full a drink! An pig he wee wee full a drink! Dis is sex-in-
step to dat beautifull soun dat deep deep down thru me
pump da danceflower. On-an-off da off-beat dat is dance,
on an-off the off beat dat is dance Pig move alone bud ta da
crawd too he belong a family-a-sorts is wad he make wid
deez happysoun fox. Pump pump pump pump oh fuck my
head ja luvly beat deep inta me an take me home ta beddy
byes an pump me more to sleep soft an loss lost . . . an still
yeah I feel da finish of dis real music. I let da music leave
da soul . . .

Sound of a poxy dance tune is faded up.

PIG. Fookchaa!! Stoodent, in a?

RUNT. Lookalike.

PIG. All dat chit-chat, chit-chat, chit-chat . . . SHAT!! Pork's brightest oud der an whod a guessed, Runt? I men, look dat yoke!

RUNT. Pig poin ta a lanky skin an bone dress in da height a ration!

PIG. Jesus da hairy an Joseph!

RUNT. He nee Runt style help! His tapioca skin globby eyes an bum hole moud all sittin lax need a mooppy hair style long since gone!

PIG. Das pugly, hey Runt!

RUNT. Dem stoodent type got no soul! Style in't in it!

PIG. Das righ, girl!

RUNT. De men dey act like ol dolls, da ol dolls do up like men! No tuck an seamed, no press liedly wid da iron.

PIG. Like yurs truly, yeah!

RUNT. Like dancin bags a Oxfam, dey no shame! Shame!

PIG. All dis chat give me a fuck a da throat!

RUNT. Pine, Pig?

PIG. Ta ta, yeah! We rob all in sied! Every nigh purrmotion nied! A liddle Smurph all alone it sit! Poor liddle lonely ting! War da mammy war da mammy?

RUNT. I'm ja mammy!

PIG *(shouts)*. Wat you lookin at??

RUNT. Tanks, pal!

They drink.

RUNT. I look a deez students yeah, I tink a all da learnin das goin in ta dem, I tink a da books dey do read all stack tall inside dem oblong heads, I tink a da exam an all, all dat A B C plus an minus F an all . . . an Pig . . .

PIG. Wad now ol girl?

RUNT. Wad do dey wanna be?

PIG. Dey wanna be der mams an dads a course!

RUNT. Wadda we wanna be, Pig?

PIG. Leff alone. Righ pal!

RUNT. Righ, Pig. Mu zack up!

Music begins. PIG *dances with a woman.* RUNT *plays the woman.*

PIG. Ja wanna dance?? Make no odds! I take her up anyhowways! I wine my charm aboud da waste! She say sometin . . . I don no dat squeak too well. She food inta me though an soon she in dance heaven! Kiss da face, will ya! On da lips, want ya! Don pull amay, hah! Owney baba cry! A full mast in da kax Pig he ready to set sail! She cry all elploss. I like ta lick da neck, yeah! Jus like a big lolly! She pinn close! Ohhhhhhh now look a da liddle titsies! Who da baba cry? Was jar name, lover?

RUNT. Liddle baby tiny tears?!

PIG. She's a terrible tease, hey Runt?

RUNT. Two hail marys an' an our father, hey sister! Les do da piggy dance, ya on!! War da fook is my man so!!

PIG. Ah pik da fucker Runt!

RUNT. So Runt move in on misty mothball! Da tapioca king is who we'll take! Up reel close! Da boy he dead ugly okay! He got stoopid all ova him. Da liddle chalky face an tacky eyes. So on-an-off da off-beat dat is dance we move . . . me an dineasaur Barney, dat is. Da boy dance like a baba who nee ta piss o jus done a piss an nee ta leave! He stick a sweety han onta my neck an mamble a squeak I don understan! He sway-in an ova, da moud come-in like a gian manhole. An den he . . .

PIG. Den he kiss Runt! An dat my queue! Ova I move! Move real fass, yeah! Scream ou loud I scream an grab da liddle fuck an Runt she say,

RUNT. He kiss me, Pig! He gay me tongue an all, ya dirty-doggy!!

PIG. An Runt she nee an Oscar for dat, yeah, I almos give a liddle applause an all but da boy he say

RUNT. Sorry boss! Hands off look!

PIG. But da damage it is *done, ya bad boy!* Oud a da door a dis poxy disco an oud onta Stoodent Straight I trow dis streaky stretch a bad bacon! See I play da par a da boyfriend, soap opera fans! Is jealous all ovur, in it! Smash! Ya fillty bollix! Smash smash smash smash smash smash smash smash!!!

PIG *beats him up.* RUNT *cheers him on for a bit.*

PIG. Goo fun, hey! Nice trick, cat woman!

RUNT. Birrday present in it?

PIG. Jar my bird day giff in life, Runt!!

RUNT. Pig the chrissy cracker! Bang bang bang bang!!

PIG. You're the one sweet ting!

RUNT. Better be better be!!

PIG. Jarr my bes pal in da whole whirl.

RUNT. Jarr my life, Pig.

PIG *grabs at* RUNT *and kisses her. She struggles and pulls away. A moment.*

PIG. Way da buzz go hun?

RUNT. Dis place pox. Les go eat yeah?

PIG. Burger baps-a- go-go!!

RUNT. Lead da way fas-boy!!

PIG *and* RUNT *in a burger place.*

PIG. Mister Kung Fu! Two Battur burgurs! Two Sauce! Two Chips! Two Peas! Two Tanora! (*Pause.*) An two fawks, Gringo!

RUNT. Our two mams all sweety an stinkin a new born babas
n' blood! I member open an look my eyes an ja see a liddle
baba in the nex bed. An dat liddle baba he look righ inta
me, yeah. Our mams all da full of happy but da new babys
say an do no-ting. We look cross da liddle-big space tween
da beds . . . I see own him an he own see me. Deez liddle
babies need no-ting else. So off home we go all packed!
An da baby houses side by side la! . . . an birrday in birrday
out . . . us togedder. An peeplah call me Sinead an call Pig
Darren but one day we war playin in da playroom be-an
animols on da farm an Darren play da Pig an I play da
Runt! An dat wuz it! An every beddy time our mams pull us
away from da odder one. 'Say night to Sinead, Darren'. But
Pig jus look ta me an ans (*Snorts an oink.*) An I noel what
he mean. So we grow up a bit at a dime an all dat dime we
silen when odders roun. No word or no-ting. An wen ten
arrive we squeak a diffren way den odders. An da hole a da
estate dey talk at us. Look nasty yeah. But me an Pig look
stray at dem. An we looka was happenin an we make a
whirl where Pig an Runt jar king an queen! Way was goin
down in dis clown-town is run by me an Pig fun fun. An Pig
look cross at me jus like he look when we were babas an he
alla say 'Les kill da town, ya on?' An I alla say – corse I'm
on –I'm ja pal, amn't I? An liddle tings we do like robbin
an stealin is a good ol feelin, yes indeedy. An we read dem
buuks on howta figh da peeplah ya hate. An Pig own has
me . . . an Runt own have him. But we make a whirl dat no
one can live sept us two. Bonny an Clyde, ya seen da
movie! Fannytastic, yeah! (*Laughs.*) But ya know, we liddle
babas no mo. Is all differen. All of a puddin, ders a real big
differ-ence.

PIG. I'd grobble all da Battur burgurs in China sept I'm struck
in dis grubby tub, hey Runt!

RUNT. Say again?

PIG. I'd grobble all da Battur burgurs in China cept I'm stuck
in dis grubby tub!

RUNT. Yeah! 'Course!

PIG. Wa do dey call Chinese takeaways in China, Runt?

RUNT. Don no!

The two sit in silence for some time. Eating.

PIG. Up up up up up up up!!

RUNT. Off homes, yeah?

PIG. Not off no! Not off but out Runt!! Not off but more more more much more!! Sa out da door an da liddle ones step out onta Patsy Street! (*Calling out.*) PORK!! Cheerio ol pal!!

RUNT. Pig?

PIG. TAXI!!

RUNT. Purr us Pig!?

PIG. We're da reel ting, ol girl! Les split dis party, yeah!

PIG *and* RUNT *in taxi.*

PIG. Crossheaven! Drive on mister cabman!!

Sound of a car.

RUNT. An off we do!

PIG. Now das reel class!

RUNT. Look how da scummy wet grey a Pork Sity spindown da plughole.

PIG. as da two speed on, an on we speed! Sa so long to dat sad song, hey Runt!!

RUNT. Up an out ova da valley, Pig!! An da black a da cuntry like a big snuggly doovey it cuddle us up reel good yeah!!

PIG. Snuggle down outta town!!

RUNT. Hey da fresh air, pal!!

PIG. Wine down da windy an drink it all in, Runt!

RUNT. Da taxi so fas dat da fresh air fill me up like a big happy ba-loon!!

PIG. Not like da stenchy piss dat we all know!

RUNT. Look a da moo moo look!!

PIG. Was me ol mam doin der, Runt!!

RUNT. Is way pass yer beddy times ya silly cow!!

PIG. So fook off home why don jaa!! On an on mister cabman!!

RUNT. On an on, an let da fas fresh air kiss an clean dis liddle girl up!!

PIG. Yer bird-day gif, Runt!

RUNT. Where Pig?

PIG. Taxi stop!

Car sounds stop.

PIG. Crossheaven, da colour a love, dis where it is hun!!

Sounds of the sea have been faded up over the above. The two look out.

RUNT. Nice.

PIG. Der ye are, pal. Das da big blue der. All dat wator, hah. Is all yers Runt.

RUNT. Mine Pig?

PIG. I got big bag in my plopet I can lash it inta. (*Laughs.*)

RUNT. Big open space an jus we standin here, Pig.

PIG. Like two specs a dust on da telly, hey girl.

RUNT. S'all calm dat move. Da sea dance up slow and down to up slow again. Is beautiful hey, Pig?

PIG. Top a da whirl, in it!

RUNT. Jesus, wad a smell!!

PIG. Salt. Salt sea smell.

RUNT. An da soun a da sea too . . .

PIG. Yeah, Rover at his doggy bowl, hey Runt?! Lap lap lap!

RUNT. I wanna walk inta da sea an neva come back. I wan ta tide to take me outa me an give me someone differen . . . maybe jus fur a halfhour or so! Dat be good, wouldn't it Pig?

PIG. Jesus Runt! Dat be impossible! A half hour, fuck! (*Pause.*)
I wanna a huge space ship rocket la, take it up to da cosmos
shiny stars all twinkle twinkle an I shit in my saucer an
have a good look down on da big big blue. Derd be a button
named Lazer dat blast all da shitty bits dat ya'd see, yeah.
I press dat button an Lazer would fireball all below an den
back down I fly to Crossheaven happy dat all das left a Pork
Sity is my roam your roam an da Palace Disco cause das all
dat matters, Runt . . . ress is jus weekday stuff.

RUNT. Da Palace Disco. Is a dream, Pig.

PIG. Pig know way da Palace is. Honest!

RUNT. Sure, Pig.

PIG (*pause*). Les go home, yeah. Beddy byes hun! Yer place
furs stop, yeah!

RUNT. No race. Les stay.

PIG. Handsome.

Long silence as the two listen to the sea.

PIG. Happy birrday taday, Runt!

RUNT. Da bes', Pig! Til nex year, hah. (PIG *nods. Pause.*) Pig?

PIG. Yes ol pal?

RUNT. Tanks! Is real nice dis.

PIG *and* RUNT *remain standing looking out at the sea. The
sound of a car horn is heard.* PIG *looks over his shoulder.*

PIG. Fuck an wait, ja langer!!

RUNT *smiles at* PIG. *They look out. Lights fade to a new
state.* PIG *and* RUNT *returning home. Music.*

RUNT: Say night to Sinead Darren!!

PIG *oinks.*

RUNT. Tomborrow evey ol pal!!

PIG. Night, Runt!!

New state. PIG *and* RUNT *watching an episode of Baywatch which we hear under music. It's the next day.*

RUNT: Jees Pig, top a da delly dis!

PIG. God it all, pal!

RUNT. Baywatch da true winner, yeah!

PIG. Soun, sea an san

RUNT. An sex too, pal!

PIG. Da four 's'is, hey Runt! (*He laughs.*)

RUNT. Oh yeah! (*She laughs. Then.*) Look a dat boy! Bronze, he a blue eye boy wid da real big beach balls, pal!

PIG. Imagine dat chunk doin da breast strokey on ol Runt, hey!

RUNT. Fook off you!

PIG. Imagine me gainst dat bloke in da race, hun! Who da winner den pal?!

RUNT. Pig a corse!

PIG. Easy peasey bronze boy! Takey ye all on, ya Caliphoney babies!!

RUNT. Oh pal, look at dat der!

PIG. Nice gaff, yeah!

RUNT. Jiff clean, Pig! Da toilea bowl all a sparkly like is Jesus Christ's very own bog. Is beautiful.

PIG. Imagine havin a wazz in dat bowl!

RUNT. Oh yeah, pal! A pock-full a tens ta wipe da bum hole an all! (*She laughs.*)

PIG. Now das class girl! (*He laughs.*)

RUNT. Imagine me born der?

PIG. An me too yeah! Two Baywatch babes, Pig an Runt!

RUNT. Hoy mam! Wat time ya call dis, daff girl!! Dat da dins?! Runt she starve but who da you care, hey?!

PIG. Tateys an gravy, yummy yummy! Shlap it der look!

RUNT. Da fookin telly, mam! Outta da fookin way, fatty!

PIG. Move it, maestro!

RUNT. Get da fook out so!

PIG. Don give up da day job, hey mammy!

RUNT. Nice woon!

PIG. Ta ta girl! (*Pause.*) Hey! Look a dat girlly there!

RUNT. Oh yeah!

PIG. Pamela Anderson!

RUNT. Beautiful. Beautiful girl!

PIG. But dat dress she wear, pal! It move like . . . like . . .

RUNT. Pig?

PIG. Like some liddle fedder ya can see fall in da sky oudda a
birdy dat fly by.

RUNT. Ohhh yeah!! (*Pause.*) Eat up, yeah!

Music. PIG *stands out.*

PIG. Why I kiss da honey lips a Runt? An now all dat I put my
gob to is Runt I take an tase. I close da eyes an see da
inhide a Runt legs. Da silk a da tighs an da liddle heaven a
panties dat sit above. Dat liddle furry tuff dat wid ma paws
I cup an knead. Runt she get all sof an moise an she gendle
press inta my han which seem to call her in . . . she come
in. An we on da floor an lick da stiff tips a tits an all da time
she on my fingur an da tongues dey disco dance an we
move da wet spit aboud our face. I feel dis da time. Pig nee
to be a man. I all caught up in da pants an zip zip Runt fold
her han aboud me. She take me oud an me all shiny an hard
I open her real sof. Open. She wet an moan. Liddle moan. I
poosh an touch da way in. An now Pig an Runt are da one.
We move an all is warm an sof wet, an da two well lost in
da sex we move slow an gendle, yeah, an Runt she giv one
mo moan an Pig he pour inta da Runt. We man an woman
now. We kiss wid tongues. Pig go nice sof inside. My liddle

baby seal wants oud. I kiss Runt eyes. She all shiny an glow as I pull-ou.

Music stops.

PIG. En ter tain ment! Ya on?!!

RUNT. Wat?

PIG & RUNT. En-ter-tain-ment!

RUNT. Now Pig?

PIG. Off out yeah!?

RUNT. Wer da bobs so!?

PIG. A few bobs, Runt! Wat ya say?!

RUNT. Tonigh, Pig! Now?

PIG. Seventeen, yeah!

RUNT. Yeah!

PIG. Well les make up to flip out, yeah?!

RUNT AND PIG. Up up up up up up up up up up up!

PIG. Raceyaso!!!

RUNT. Fook yes!!

Sounds of Provo Bar faded up.

PIG. Hoy Marky!

RUNT. So back in da provo pub purr a secon nigh surprise yeah, an we in nee a da drink. Solids come in da shape of a scampi fries which Pig do hate but I do adore. So in da drinky fish mush my belly bubble an lisson as Pig wine up Marky an play da liddle bad boy! When all of a puddin

PIG. Get a gawk at that yoke! Is a fookin karaokee! Hoy Markie, was dis, boy? Charity funk or wat?!!

RUNT. It's a Cork Sinn Fein do!

PIG. Say Markie, under another of his mam's *TANG TOPS!!*

RUNT. Wid dat da doors a da pub flap op an close as da Sinn Fein army pile-in an gadder bout da stout taps! Five

hundred a da bas-turds all in nees of a good shave an da
girlfrens like cocker spaniels come in oudda da rain! Da
place go crazy!!

*Sounds of extremely busy pub an somebody singing Danny
Boy.*

PIG. Ere, shouldn't ya be out plantin bombs an beaten up ol
ladies, ya fookin weirdos!!

RUNT. Fair dues, boy.

PIG. Pine, girl?

RUNT. Bag a scamp too, yeah!

PIG. So at da bar I mee da Karaokee-man himself of which I
fine his name is Trevor. So Trevor, I say to dis small speccy
spec-a-fuck, how match a go, hey man!? Trevor say, it's
free. Dat righ Trev? Trouble is, says Trevor, only Provo
songs tonigh ol pal! Really Trev? A fiver saw Trevor all righ
for a surprise for my girl, yeah das her wid da packet a
Scampi, a course she's nice, Trev-boy, she beautiful her!

RUNT. Oh get da fook off da stage, ape man!

PIG. Real lady, Trev!

RUNT. A crease ball wanders over. Da girlfren a Danny Boy it
seem! 'I'll fuckin claim ya if ya don shift yer hole righ
now!', says she. I stan up. Smell da cheap fume frum way
under da Martini. Her chip paper skin wid drawn on eyes an
lips dat lookalike well dangerous skidmarks. I face dis ugly
puss an holdin a fist full a scampi fry I mash it inta her gob!
When SHLAP!! (RUNT *reacts to punch in the face.*) She
pack a punch dis doll! SSMACKKK!! (*Reacts the same.*)
Opens up da nose an blood all drip drip drop from da Runt!
She hold hold a my hair an spit da scampi mush back inta
my face an onta da fancy top I do wear. Dat stain won' shif
too easy, I tink! FUCKKKKK!!! (*Reacts.*) Where Pig?
Where ya now Mister Kissy!? Mister Kissy! Mister Kissy!
Mister kissy! Mister Kissy!!

Be my Baby by The Ronettes comes on. PIG *performs it
Karaokee style miming to the original. Meanwhile* RUNT
is seen to be reacting to some violent punches to her face.
PIG *finishes mid song.*

PIG. Runt?

RUNT. Outside, pal!

RUNT *turns to* PIG. *Blood pours from her face.*

PIG. Wat mess! Look dat beat up face!

RUNT. Les ship out, yeah!

PIG. I fuckin burn da fuck who did dis! Who did, poin da way!
   Won' take long o no-ting! Justice see der face smash in!
   Who, Runt, who hey?

RUNT. No figh no more!

PIG. Lie back an die is dat da chant, Runt!

RUNT. Off home, yeah!

PIG. Is dis not Pig an Runt side by side remembers? A silen
   deal is wad we may way back in sain fridgets ward, we join,
   remembers, an in dat look we set out Runt, you an me pal,
   to make us king an queen a Pork Sity!

RUNT. Leave!

PIG (*pause*). Yeah ol pal, leave! Les leave all dat scum to dat
   scum!! An nows breed it in pal! Breed in Pork's own poxy
   air. Elp sued da cut an bruise ya da have, Runt. Jees Runt
   wadda fook dat, hey! Sorry pal! Jus stay in real calm an
   Pig he put tings righ, hey! Smar boy!! So no tears liddle
   one! . . . please! (*Puts his hand over her eyes and covers
   his eyes with his other hand.*) Calm mother, calm! An sleep
   an res, ol sweet ting! Calm liddle pretty skin. (*Lowers his
   hands from her eyes.*)

RUNT. Oh my gian fuck of a beautiful white marbly mosque!
   Is da Palace. Is da Palace Disco.

PIG. Oh my guardy angel ya come up trumps dis time fella!!!

RUNT. How did dis big white house dat mus be da size a da Pork ferry ta poxy England, how did dis gaff play hide-an-seek purr dis long, pal? Is Pork dat big?

PIG. Not big no but manky. Not big Runt bud a big black barrel a black dat only do pause purr da pissy grey rain. Bud ya know, ol girl, even a great big poo poo has its diamonds an dis great big great marbly monstrosity which you did righly call da size of da Pork ferry, dis is Pork's own liddle gem!

RUNT. It take a Captain Cook like my very own bes pal ta sniff it out, hey! Wat a tresure you bot are! Dis is really it, Pig!

PIG. Oh no pal, dis is much more dan it! Ya know where da top stops, well dis stop . . .

RUNT. . . . is one step on top of dat top! Dis is like da cream cept beighy creamyer!

PIG. One hundred per cent don tell da true facs here, Runt!

RUNT. Dis is bettur den gold.

PIG. Da pick a da bunch!

RUNT. Champain,

PIG. Ta everyone elses Fanta! Man United,

RUNT. Ta everyone elses West ham!

PIG. Ya noel wen Sonia finally become champion da wonder horse an gallop her way to suckycess bak in ol Godden-burg, yeah? An Sonia stan on da winny po-dium wid da whirl medal all a dangle from da pretty liddle neck as da nationalist rant-hymn blast da fuck oudda da sky an da green white an porridge all a flutter in da breeze. An all da Irish aroun da track an in da whirl, an anybod who even fuck an Irish dey all have a liddle tear a boy in der eye when dey say, 'dis is a great day for Our-land!' Well Runt, dis is a bettur day!

RUNT. Fuck, yes!!

PIG *and* RUNT *go to enter the Palace.*

RUNT. Stop!

PIG *stops.*

PIG. Ah bollix!

RUNT. A gian cyclops a bricks wid bouncer tatooes on his toilea face.

PIG. Jus my luck, hey! So wers Hans gone, ol Chew-back-a?!

RUNT. Regular are ya?

PIG. Once in da moring an again in da evening, doctur!

RUNT. Pig too smart fur dis tic toc! Da man he screw up da face an lookalike a playt a mash an mushy pea sept a bit more starchey. He look down na Pig an he say, 'I think you know my little brother.'

PIG. Who he fat man?

RUNT. He worked down in the off licence in Blackpool! But now he's on the dole.

PIG. Das a sad an sorry story.

RUNT. I watch Pig as da past tap em on da shold wid a hi-dee-hi. Off licence. Blackcruel. Fuck me.

PIG. Yeah I noel Foxy, good bloke yeah!

RUNT. Bud da big man no who Pig is.

PIG. He place his shovel han onta ma head an den he say

RUNT. I hate the little bollix, myself!

PIG (*laughs*). Tank fuck! (*Both laugh.*)

RUNT. Excuse me, so what's the password, then?

PIG. Sorry boss? Password? Is that wat you say ol boy? Was da password, yeah?

RUNT. You know, what's the colour of love?

PIG (*pause*). Wad sorra love?

RUNT. The sort of love that you feel. The sort of love that only one colour can tell you about. The sort of love that can pick you up with a stupid grin cut ear to ear and can then cut your throat just as easily. (*Pause.*) An I look a Pig. An Pig he loss jus like da Runt is. Wad we know, hey? We all alone on da Palace Disco step wid Foxy's big pox of a brud. Seems like hours tic-by an Pig he jus look an stare straight ahead. (*Pause.*) An den, Pig, frum somewers he say

PIG. Blue. Blue da colour a love. Is blue, yeah?

RUNT. An da big double decker in da pink dicky bow wave his kingsize han an say,. Cloakroom on the left.

Music up. They're in. PIG *goes for the drinks.*

PIG. Pine, pal?

RUNT. G and T, yeah yeah!!

PIG. Ohhhhhhhhhh righhhhhh, hasta be, hasta be, Jo-Hannah Lum-mel-lee!!

RUNT. An a pak a Scampi Fries, Pig!

PIG. Three paks in dis side a heaven, girl!

RUNT. *Three* Pig!??

PIG. Dis a free cuntry, ol girl! Is yer want ta suck on dose liddle poxy fishy tings dat remind me a Nero's balls or sum schlop ya put out fur a liddle hungry kitty kat, yeah!! Runt ol pal, yer wish is my demand!

RUNT. My hero!

PIG. I fuck off so!

PIG *gets the drinks in.* RUNT *alone. Looks about.*

RUNT. So Runt she touchdown on all da chrome an da sky blue draylon! Who'd a guesst? Pig wid da righ ans fur Foxy's big brud an open sess me an Pig in a Cinderella ball, yeah, cept no sad old Billa or anythin panto, tank fuckin Jesus! Surprise surprise! Fur a sec I tink, hey mayb all dat drink drink play sum sorta shake it all abou insize my beautiful liddle head so I do da pinch an den da eyes all

close den peep-op again an . . . an is true. Me in da Palace
Disco!! Seventeen!!! All grow up! True story no fict!

PIG. Das three packs, yeah! Three! Fur da ol doll!

RUNT. All da beautys in here! All dancin good da on an off
beat dat in real real dance! I spy sumthin begins wid
Princess! She in black chambray dress fit an flare mid-calf,
seamed. She know da fash! Real nice job! An I tink me as
her dancin wid all da frens, yeah! All laughin, all dancin da
same as one! Maybe we dress before in my room! Mayb we
chit chat an I say, I don fancy, Frankie, no, ohhh does it
really show? An we all laugh an gozzel back another boddle
a Ritz! No gozzel, no, sip! An we at da Palace Disco fun
fun fun an jus maybe dis bloke dream cum true who look
like Phil Babb or sum odder hunk mayb he say nice dress
an I say, tank you, I made it myself an he kiss my han an
not try to tickle my insize wid his Tayto tongue! Mayb dat
be good! Mayb dat be good fun jus ta try, ya know!

PIG. Remarkable in it! I mean look at dat daycor, Runt, few
bob der I'd say! Real class, all righ! Imagine dis yer gaff!
Cept da prices mayb-a cheepur a course!

RUNT. Cheers, pal!

PIG. To you, hun!

RUNT. Who'd a guesst, hey?

PIG. All fur one!

RUNT. Yeah das righ. (*Sees something in front of her.*) Ders a
mirror look!

PIG. Who dat beautiful pair?

RUNT. Us a course!

PIG. Like a misty an misses, Runt!

RUNT. Zact same. (*Pause.*) An Pig an Runt sit in da big bubble
dat is my life! Seventeen years an fuck all chane. Pig still
look ta me an dat look keep me in Pig-step! Runt da real
runt in dis liddle carriage. Well, up up up up up up up up up
up up up up up up up , get up girl! Is yer choice, party girl!!

PIG. Was dis!?

RUNT (*pause*). Toilea.

PIG. Ja wan more a da Scampi ta soak it all up?

RUNT. Tanks bud no tanks.

PIG. Maybe up latur an show off da piggy dance, ya on?!

RUNT. Maybe, yeah!

PIG. Handsome!! (*Pause.*) An Runt off, leave da Pig in wat be a well ol feelin, yah yah! See I wan da buzz, yeah! Look les stop all dis chitty chat shat an les sees whos da number plum aroun here! Dey all look an laugh a me! Hear dem?!! I can see it, yeah! Dey loads a cash an look a Pig an, who he, dey say! Who'd da liddle boy in da a confirmation suity?? Well, Fuck anuff! I all calm fur *she* know who, but no more! Dis no me, no!! Pig he wan ta balance it righ an da Palace Disco need a less an Pig he da real teach tonigh, all righ! So who da furs hey?

RUNT. Tank you, I made it myself!

PIG. Was dis! Oh yes! Jus like before, yeah! Good ol Runt! She play da girlfren an misty Pig he play da boyfren! But dis time I read da message purr real! She wan *us* purr real! Me an her! We jar it! We fucking jar ya know!

RUNT *holds out her hand which we imagine is being kissed.*

PIG. An thru da pump pump pump a da disco dance I see it all! Pig on his marks an all set as misty hansome move in on Runt an

RUNT. Kiss my hand.

PIG. An das my queue!!! Ova I move! Move real fass, yeah! Scream ou loud I scream an grab da liddle fuck an Runt she say,

RUNT. Jesus Pig no! No!!!

PIG. Oud oud oud oud oud oud OUD OUD OUD!!!!!! Take oud! Move oudda da fuckin way! Door open shut! Throw! You dirty liddle fuck she my girlfren bollix! Smash! Kassshhh! Open da nose da eye! Blood blood blood! An Smashhh smasshhh smash! I am da king ya fuckidy fuck!

Ashtray! Smash kaasshhhh head smasshhh! Head crack op!
She mine, luvver boy! She my girl! Me an her, king an
queen ya bad boy! Scream baby liddle baby scream an
SMASH SMASH SMASH . . . SMASHHH!!!!!

RUNT. Oh fuck.

PIG. Dead hun, jus like an action flic! Big mess dis!

RUNT. Cheerio. So-long pal.

PIG. Wat? Stay! (*Overlapping.*) STAY STAY STAY STAY
STAY STAY STAY!!!!

RUNT (*overlapping*). GO GO GO GO GO GO GO GO GO!!
An Runt race good dis time! Mus ged away! No mo all dis
play an pain! So so-long to all dat pox! Go girl! Leave! An
it well ovur, drama fans! Runt race her ways up da piss-grey
straight wid da Palace Disco an poor ol Pig on her back! Jus
me! Jus da liddle girl all aloneys! An still I see Pig like he
besie me, yeah. He my one an only, he da bes an da worse
pal in dis bad ol whirl. An I wan Pig an I wan for all da
buzz an all da disco we do dance but hey ho an wadda ya
know I wan fur sumthin else! Sumthin differen! Sumthin
differen! Fuckin freedom!! Jus me!! Jus da Runt!! So mayb
ta Crossheaven, mayb das where a girl can sleep sleep sleep
an be alone. Jus me an da big big colour blue. Dat colour
blue! (*Pause.*) An Runt take a breeder on Christy's Ring . . .
an I look a da sun creep up on my pal Pork . . . *Cork*. An
da sun it really is a beautiful big thing (*Pause.*) An Runt she
alone now. But is okay now, is all righ. (*Pause.*) Runt, she
calm, calm down . . . an I watch . . . da liddle quack
quacks . . . I look . . . at the ducks . . . as they swim in
the morning sun . . . in the great big . . . . watery-shite . . .
that is the river Lee.

Where to?

Light slowly fades down on PIG *until out.*

Then light slowly fades down on RUNT.

Blackout.

The end.

SUCKING DUBLIN

Characters

LITTLE LAMB

STEVE

AMANDA

FAT

LEP

Sucking Dublin was first produced by the Outreach Department
of the Abbey Theatre, Dublin, in September 1997,
with the following cast:

LITTLE LAMB	Deirdre Molloy
STEVE	Anto Nolan
AMANDA	Morna Regan
FAT	Linda Gough
LEP	Aiden Kelly

Directed by Sarah Thornton
Designed by Aedin Cosgrove

A chorus of five were played by members of the Youth Reach
Centres of Ballymun, Ballyfermot, Basin Lane and North
Great Georges Street

The play was workshopped for a week prior to rehearsal

Lights flick on to full. Loud dance music coincides with this.
We are in a tiny flat beautifully furnished in all white. This is
STEVE *and* AMANDA's *council flat in Dublin City. They host*
an eighteenth birthday party which is well under way.

LITTLE LAMB. I fuckin love this one.

STEVE. Oh yes.

LITTLE LAMB. Turn it up.

STEVE. Burst the fuckin eardrums! Keep it down.

AMANDA. Have you got a drink?

FAT. Yeah.

STEVE. She's eatin us out of house an home, int she . . .

AMANDA. Stop!!

STEVE. She's got an awful lip on her too!

AMANDA. There's plenty!

STEVE. I'm only messin! Here Fat eat up.

LITTLE LAMB. I'm locked!!

FAT. I know!

LITTLE LAMB. No I'm really locked! I mean I was pissed
    earlier but I'm fucked now!

FAT. Happy birthday!!

STEVE. Yeah happy birthday love.

LITTLE LAMB. Eighteen for God sakes.

STEVE. Look more like fourteen dun she?

AMANDA. Good looks are in the family!

LITTLE LAMB. We're all rides!

STEVE. Listen to that!

AMANDA. Fuckin true!

STEVE. Looked in the mirror lately!

AMANDA. Can't get you away from the thing!

LITTLE LAMB. He's handsome though isn't he?

AMANDA. Movie star looks.

STEVE. That's right!

AMANDA. Yeah Lassie!

STEVE. Two bitches in the one flat then!

AMANDA. Sharp aren't ya?

STEVE. Cut you're bleedin throat!

LITTLE LAMB. Am I the only one gettin locked here?

FAT. Not likely!

LITTLE LAMB *looks down on* LEP *collapsed on the couch.*

LITTLE LAMB. He's fucked isn't he?

FAT. You know what he gets like.

LITTLE LAMB. I love him.

FAT. I know.

LITTLE LAMB. Brilliant when he gets going.

FAT. He's a laugh alright.

LITTLE LAMB. He's like our little baby sleeping there.

FAT. Puke stains an all!

LITTLE LAMB *kisses him on the forehead.* STEVE *appears from behind the couch wearing devils horns. He roars into* LEP'*s face.*

LITTLE LAMB. Fuckin hell!

FAT. Jesus!

STEVE. Wake up ya lazy bollox!!

LITTLE LAMB. Steve!

LEP. Wha?

STEVE *roars into his face again.*

LEP. Fuckin hell!! What's that?

STEVE. It's the devil isn't it?!

LEP. Steve??

STEVE. The head on him! See that Lamb? Scare the shite out of him!

LEP. Mad man!

STEVE *roars into his face again.*

LEP. Get fuckin off ya spastic! Jesus! He's mad Amanda!

AMANDA. Tell me about it!

LEP. Shit me knickers there!

STEVE. Not on my couch ya won't!

LITTLE LAMB (*laughing*). I think I'm going ta piss me pants!

STEVE. Not the bleedin two a yas!

LEP. It's your doin man!

LITTLE LAMB. Oh stop!!

FAT. Can I use your jacks?

STEVE. Fuckin right ya can!

AMANDA. Out through there.

FAT *exits.*

STEVE. Imagine that yoke crapping on the carpet! Build a roundabout to get around it!

LITTLE LAMB. Ah stop!

LEP. That's my big sis you're slaggin!

STEVE. Shut up you or it's back on with the horns!

Sounds of a large crowd shouting 'OUT OUT OUT' are heard outside the door.

AMANDA. Ah for fuck's sakes!

LITTLE LAMB. Jesus Christ!

STEVE. Ignore that!

AMANDA. Are you serious?!

LITTLE LAMB. When did this all start?

STEVE. They'll be sorted out!! Don't worry about that!!

AMANDA. Started yesterday!

LITTLE LAMB. Fuckin hell!! S'like a film now or somethin!! They've got torches, look!

LEP. Y'all be burnt at the stake, Steve! Not long now, pal!

STEVE. Just ignore it all right!!

AMANDA. You were meant ta get it sorted, Steve!!

STEVE. Shut yer fuckin trap!

LITTLE LAMB. Go on, Steve!

STEVE goes to the door. There are locks all the way down. He shouts out.

STEVE. Would ya all fuck off home now!! Should be all tucked up in yer beddy byes, ya bleedin weirdos!!

LEP. Go on, ya mad man!!

STEVE. Look it, there's no drugs here, pal!! This flat is pure!! Yer barkin up the wrong tree, lads!! This is a drug free zone, (*To* AMANDA.) is that what they call it?

AMANDA. Yeah!

STEVE (*shouts*). Drug free!! Apart from the wife's valium!

AMANDA. Tell the fuckin world why don't ya!

STEVE. Come on then!! Smash down the door!! Ya'd need twelve pound of Semtex ta shift that door!! Solid steel look!! (*Hammers the door with his hand.*)

Sounds from outside suddenly stop. Silence.

STEVE. What about that!

LITTLE LAMB. Fuckin hell!

STEVE. Untouchable!

AMANDA. What a rock star!!

STEVE. A little bit of gentle persuasion, Lamb!

AMANDA. They'll be back soon enough!

STEVE. Am I the only one gettin locked here?!

LITTLE LAMB. Not fuckin likely!!

STEVE. Down the hatch and out yer gaash!

LITTLE LAMB (*screams*). Presents!!!

AMANDA. You got them!

LITTLE LAMB. Is that it? Poxy chain!

AMANDA. Ya little bitch!

STEVE. Cost a packet.

LITTLE LAMB. A packet of Tayto maybe!

AMANDA. You know what to do with it sis!

LITTLE LAMB. Messin!!

AMANDA. Better be!

LITTLE LAMB. Jesus! Relax on the jacks Amanda!

STEVE. Not with that yoke in there!

AMANDA (*answering* LITTLE LAMB). Yeah!

STEVE. I've got you something else.

LITTLE LAMB. What?

STEVE. It's something small now!

LITTLE LAMB. Come on give us it.

STEVE. Wrapped it meself.

Hands her a teddy bear without any wrapping on it.

LITTLE LAMB. Oh Jesus!!

STEVE. Cute isn't it!

LITTLE LAMB. It's lovely! Ah look only the one eye!!

STEVE. One of a kind! Got someone to look for it specially!

LITTLE LAMB. Deadly isn't he!

AMANDA. Am I the only one gettin locked here!?

LITTLE LAMB. Not fuckin likely!!

FAT enters.

STEVE Back then?

FAT. What do you think?

STEVE. I could feel a planet move into the room alright!

FAT. That's very funny.

STEVE. No it's not!

FAT. You're right it's just crap!

STEVE. I was thinkin sad! How sad it all is!

FAT. Thinkin, now when did you pick that up Einstein?

STEVE. Everyone allright then!!

LITTLE LAMB. Lovely Steve!!

STEVE. Enjoyin yourself?

LITTLE LAMB. I'm locked am'nt I?

STEVE. You look beautiful!

LITTLE LAMB. That's because I'm a fuckin ride!

STEVE. You're right.

LITTLE LAMB. Is he alright?

STEVE. He's wasted. Best place for him isn't it?

LITTLE LAMB. Do you love my sister?

STEVE. What?

LITTLE LAMB. You heard what I said! Do you love Amanda?

STEVE. What the fuck do you think?

LITTLE LAMB. Do ya?

STEVE. Are you teasin me?

LITTLE LAMB. Don't be gettin angry! Answer the question.
   Do ya fancy her even?

STEVE. I'll put the song on again?

LITTLE LAMB. Dance with her will ya?

STEVE. Whose party is this?

LITTLE LAMB. S'mine.

STEVE. That's right.

LITTLE LAMB. So?

STEVE. Anyone I'll dance with, Lamb . . . it's you babe!
   Yeah??

LITTLE LAMB. Come on so!

'Happy Birthday to Ya' is blasted up too high. STEVE
*screams out the chorus of 'Happy Birthday to Ya' and
begins to dance with* LITTLE LAMB. *They tease one
another with the party blowers blowing them into each
other's face. Sounds of 'Out Out Out' from outside the flat
are heard.* STEVE *suddenly kisses her and holds her tight
into him. She folds into him, pissed and giggling.* STEVE
*suddenly loses it and kisses her more, feeling her up
and placing her on the coffee table. Her sitting with her
back to the audience.* STEVE *gets down and begins to rape*
LITTLE LAMB. *She calls out* LEP's *name. She flops down
on the coffee table her head facing the audience.* STEVE's
actions are clumsy and lost but he goes at it really hard.
AMANDA *looks on completely petrified.* FAT *stands above*
STEVE *and* LITTLE LAMB. STEVE *stops and pulls away.*
LITTLE LAMB *stands up and begins to cry. The song
finishes but the sounds of 'Out Out Out' build.* LITTLE

LAMB *wanders over to the door and begins to unlock the locks. She opens the door and exits.* FAT *and* LEP *also exit.* STEVE *remains seated on the couch. Sounds fade out as* AMANDA *locks the door and begins to clean up.*

Light fades up on FAT *and* LEP. *Sounds of bus.* FAT *tucks into a plastic bag full of assorted cakes.* LEP *is completely wired. He rocks in his chair for a bit sensing that he is about to explode at any moment. Then he does.*

LEP. EXPLODE!!! EXPLODE!!! EC-STA-CEEEEEE!!!!! (*To audience.*) What a fuckin laugh what a fuckin laugh what a fuckin laugh what a fuckin laugh!!! Life is a laugh!! Life is a great big fat fart of a fat laugh and guess who's laughin? Who's the man who's the man? Fuckin me, for sure!! My little white tab rattlin about me jukebox!! 'Early mornin wake up call, mister Lep!!' Lep my name!! My name short for Leper!! Is on the seat, look!! And look who beside too! My Little Lamb!! Lep loves Little happy birthday Lamb!! Black marker through the seat green like a lazy black river. I read me scrawl!! Little love heart!! Ahhhhhhhh isnn't that lovely!! (*Breathes in slowly and blurts out.*) Not a bus not a bus not a bus not a bus!! *This is not a bus!!* Fares pleaseeeeeeee!!! Wide awake and feelin it!! Spongey pours suckin it all in!! Livin in the moment before the cum!! Just before the big cum!! Cum cum cum!! Set me off to bed mammy!!! Whistle out a lullaby daddy!! Mammy daddy gone gone gone!! They're well gone! They runaway, yeah!! (*Laughs.*) Just me and my sis Fat now, not on a bus to fuck knows where!! From smelly death-trap flat-shat to hop on a bus but not a bus!! Where to oh fat sister of mine? No easy answer!! Just follow the Fat till I run outta me and end up peeled off this fuckin floor at the end of an evenin by some sad, very sad, cleaner-type woman who takes home two pence at the end of the week!! 'Expect me to raise a family on two pence a week, ah for fuck sake boss!!!' (*Breathes in slowly and blurts out.*) Steve! Steve!! See him yet??! Steve is God!! My life in those slinky hands that always smell of his spunk – he fingers me a little!! Fuck me over til I ask for more HEROIN – MY HERO!! Death plays table tennis! A bat in each hand!! Me – fuckin armless!! Oh referee!

Referee please! Not a fair match not a fair match!! Death –
he does a deadly top spin swerve!! A ball-a-gear fired up it
swerves Lep's way inta me gaping gob! Swallow and suck
deep and down! Lep he staggers a little stagger and stand up
as Death smash home more and more and much much more
HEROIN!! This is no contest, Death screams!! As me laugh
it all in cause life's a laugh! Life's a fuckin laugh!!!
Gobblin' up Steve's gear!! Gobblin' up Steve's gear!! No
memories just now!! What ya see is what your lookin at!
What ya get is what ya deserve!! *YOU DESERVE ME!!*
Forget me and I'll peep up and smash open your gaff, grab
your telly, rape your granny, marry your poxy daughter, ruin
your fuckin sad clean life cause you left me with nothin
cept this!! We're gettin bigger addin up addin up! There's
fuckin piles of us dirty rotten sad cunts, you could fill the
sky so all ya see is decay! DECAY!! Wouldn't that be
lovely when you're takin in your milk in the mornin!?
Fuckin sure!! Each one you ignore floats up and fills the
sky! A trip down the classy Deli dodgin the weirdos dodgin
my sorry junkie-mates, 'Excuse me!' and ten other bodies
float to that great big heap in the sky! That stank stank
stank!!! What's that smell on your shoes? That's little ol'
me!! The little bit of shite that clings to the hairs in your
bumhole? – me again, waitin for your fingers to close in and
CLOSE!! Pluck!! 'Flush me down and I'll bubble-back
sweeetheart!!!' You deserve this!! Ya want a fuckin
surprise?? I'll fuckin surprise ya!! EXPLODE!!!

Sounds out.

Fade up light on LITTLE LAMB *sitting on a red plastic
seat. She holds an exhausted cheese burger. Beside her is
her pram with her baby in it. Under the loud noise of a busy
fast food restaurant we can hear* LITTLE LAMB *crying.
The sounds fade down but remain and we join a very
distressed girl.*

LITTLE LAMB. It's all so blurry! Like I'm lookin through a
pint full a beer! 'Cept it's full a my poxy tears! A worn out
bit a toilet roll wet with snot and cryin' and cryin' and
cryin'! I should stick it in the ash tray, fuck it on the floor,
do somethin, but it keeps me thinkin about somethin else

when I don't wanta think about what I just done at home!
So stupid but all of a sudden this soggy snot rag's become
a best pal! (*Laughs a bit.*) Where's me ma! I wan me ma!
I wan a hug an a kiss, a mug an a biscuit! 'Slap on the
toaster, we're stayin in, what is it love? Talk to me, you're
me daughter!' I can't ma! Don't go feelin sad for me, ma,
or I'll fuckin burst ya!! (*Slight pause.*) I look aat me ma
and see Steve's angry face. (*Slight pause.*) Jaysus I'm
fuckin cryin' again! Send for the plumber, look at the state a
dat young one! Hands up who's a scaredy bollix? The little
girl in the burger shop with the liddle baby pram! My little
Dove – my baby – calm your mammy down with a little
grin! Go on! You're a little beaut! Ya are ya know! Ya fuckin
are! Claudia Schieffer's shaken in her boots! She is an all!
I could nearly eat ya up . . . cept you're all I've got little
baby! Well almost. (*Slight pause.*) What a mess this all is,
Dove. I can feel another flood poppin up to say 'hello'.
(*She breaks a bit off her burger and feeds it to* DOVE.)
Here ya are love! Get your gums around this muck!! Look
at those little hands of yours, hah? Just like your daddy with
your soft maulin hands!! An ya got my nose, don't ya?!
(*To herself.*) God love you!! And your chin, would ya look
at that chin!! Just like Lep's too!! Ya beaut!! (*Slight pause.
Takes a bite of the burger and grimaces.*) Our flat seems
further and further away. I can see the place for what it is
now that we're movin. Me mam starin at the spotless
cooker afraid ta leave the flat and out into the horrible
mess all around outside. And Gerard's suitcase in his room
crammed full of hopes and dreams but too scared to take the
chance . . . he's sorta happy waitin for Man United to line
out once a week and trash another useless fuckin team . . .
makes him feel like a someone. And dad skivin off work
and tellin us we're gettin out a the flat!! Wavin his savins
and promisin us the world on five hundred pounds. I spent
the last few weeks walkin in the stank grey around the flats
hatchin some sneaky plan that didn't look like I ever would.
An I seen an eleven year old playing with needles where I
used play ball, an I seen men who look like sad dogs walkin
about with nowhere to go, an I seen women workin all day
long for no money . . . just been kept busy, an I seen me in

the middle of it all with dreams of something new, maybe.
An I took that money off das and I ran and ran and ran, an
I feel like a sneaky little cunt who just shat all over her
family. An I know it's bad but it's the first right thing I ever
done. Have ta leave. So we're out me and you. Little Lamb
and her baby Dove. No more tears little one. I promise.
Let's leave this Crap Donalds and fuck off into the night.
Let's go little one.

LITTLE LAMB *gets up and leaves. Two girls sitting behind
her begin to comment.*

GIRL 1. See that?

GIRL 2. The poor thing.

GIRL 1. It's sad isn't it? Lonely.

GIRL 2. Not really. I mean I've seen sadder.

GIRL 1. Sad though.

GIRL 2. Yeah. (*Pause.*) What d'ya make of the burgers?

GIRL 1. Robbery.

GIRL 2. Yeah. Now that's really sad, Jackie, isn't it?

GIRL 1. S'pose yeah.

GIRL 2. Still, eat up.

Lights off and up on STEVE *and* AMANDA. STEVE *is
seated on the couch with the remnants of the party from the
night before.* AMANDA *is cleaning around him with a
hand-held vacuum cleaner. We watch this for a few minutes
with tremendous tension between the two.*

AMANDA. You've always had it. People would look up to
you. You scare the fuck out of me – but you can dress.
Mornin stinks of my fear and your Old Spice! Even your
skidmarks shine! You're a ride because you're different.
While all the others murdered a bag of chicken nuggets, you
had your sights on steak. I'd give me right arm for those
cheek bones. You could loosen your belt. Yeah, let's stay in
and snuggle in front of the new gas fire – ours that you
bought with your well earned cash. I'll give you a foot
massage and work upwards.

Long pause.

STEVE. Put my music on – take your knickers off – let's stay in and talk.

AMANDA begins to take her knickers off as The Flower Duet from Lakme the opera is heard at full. She sits opposite him waiting for something to happen. He completely ignores her. Fade out music after thirty seconds.

Lights and sounds fade off LITTLE LAMB *and* DOVE *and up on* LEP *who is harrassing someone.*

LEP. Ridin. D'ya ever want to though!? D'ya get the urge! I fuckin respect you, I do! Bein a fuckin nun is a brutal job, oh yeah! I seen the Sound A Music! Who's ta say if Julie Andrews was right!? She wanted her hole, am I right Sister!? All that runnin up and down mountains and ridin bikes!! Fuckin gummin for it she was!! D'ya ever get fed up with people callin ya Sister? Cause yer not everyone's sister how the fuck can ya be? 'Less yer old man lived for his bit of pokey pokey! Did he, Sister??! Gis a look under that veil-yoke! Go on, I triple dare! Baldy, are ya?! Go on gis a look!! Pope isn't fuckin lookin or nothin!! Probably ridin some African slave with tits like rain clouds, yeah?! But what if there is no God and you've just been put on this earth by the devil to piss us all off? Does that keep ya awake at night, does it Sister? Well it fuckin should ya know!!

LEP has been trying to light a wet cigarette butt that he has found on the floor. He can't do it. At the end of the speech he shouts,

LEP. FUCK THIS!!

He holds his head in his hands and cries.

A BOY *and a* GIRL *pass by* LEP *on the bus the boy turns to* LEP.

BOY. See you, you'd want to get your head examined! I got a cousin like that, he turned into a spa!

GIRL. Come on will ya!

BOY. So will ya?

GIRL. What?

BOY. Marry me.

GIRL. Too young.

BOY. Will ya ever though?

GIRL. S'pose.

BOY. Look! What do you want out of life?

GIRL. Everything good.

BOY. Everything?

GIRL. Do I look cheap to you?

BOY. You're a fucking angel.

GIRL. Respect. I like that.

Fade up on STEVE *who stands alone in the flat. Sounds of people shouting Out Out Out are heard once more. He walks over to the door and stands with his back to the door.*

Noise of the city bellowing up and down in volume as lights fade up on an extremely frightened LITTLE LAMB *as she 'walks'. The noises take on a strong rhythmic beat. Sounds of footsteps, talking, cars, sirens, various radio stations (one of which plays The Flower Song from Lakme at one point). We hear Larry Gogan's Just a Minute quiz which indicates the time as noonish.*

LITTLE LAMB. Dublin is bubblin away like yesterday's oxtail soup!! The city's actin like some mad spa all of a sudden!! Violence is ticklin the air ya can almost singalong with the fuckin thing!!

BLOKE 1. Move it ya fuckin, bitch!!

SLAPPER 1. Get the fuck home, will ya mammy!!

SLAPPER 2. The state a that young one!!

LITTLE LAMB. Me an my babe Dove, quiet an fast, our eyes down, steer through the jeers and dodge the squealin slappers with faces like dogs' raw arses.

SLAPPER 3. Watch where you're goin, ya spastic!!

LITTLE LAMB (*reacting*). Oh look Dove, a talkin arse!! Look you, ya little cunt, move over, all right?!! The mad junkie eyes on her, Dove, always suckin ya in!! Fuckin loser! We head down Westmoreland Street, the smell a the kip!! How can Dublin be the way it is, hey Dove!? One side it's all polite an money money more money! The otherside thick with gammy grey pigeons and pockets full of nothin!! An guess where we're facin to? Answers on a poxy postcard!!

GIRL. That baby should be indoors!!!

LITTLE LAMB. Then move outta the way, can't ya?!!

GIRL. Spare us some change, will ya!!

LITTLE LAMB. Do I look like a Samaritan? I don't think so!! Get your hands off the pram!!

GIRL. Ya little whore!!

LITTLE LAMB. Jesus Christ!! I wanna be floatin down the Grafton Street with the air conditionin' blowin me to and fro and makin me window shop when *I* really know and *they* really know it's all a big wish! Shops with insides that not even a brilliant painter could paint! Beautiful! Where the people that serve ya look like super models 'cept human and kind. Ya know, ya can sorta feel normal when you're not walkin about with 'shame' for company.

BLOKE 2. Look the little ride, Decco!!

BLOKE 3. The smell a the bengy off ya!!

BLOKE 2. Dishin it out are ya?!!

BLOKE 3. Get over here and sit on his face, will ya gorgeous?!!

LITTLE LAMB (*reacting*). Shite on his face more like!! I spin past that deadly kebab place where spas happily eat dog sandwiches, 'Once there's curry on it, pal!' Sorta makes me feel good lookin at those sad cavemen!! They murder-back that many crinkly chips they're all beginnin ta crinkle around the edges themselves! (*Pause.*) Over the bridge and

all that's now in front is the great big bollix of a car park
that is O' Connell Street!! The pram wheels got a life a their
own all of a sudden! Like Dove's drivin me outta the muck
ta somewhere brighter. Times like this ya wanna be the
strongest man in the universe, don't ya Dove?! Roll up
Talbot Street, peel back Abbey Street like a long forgotten
scab and fuck the two of them in a big blue bin, because ya
can, because they're so, so crap, an black, an dull, an
dangerous doorways, an secret killin' eyes, an so fuckin
dangerous! Doesn't seem fair that a river can mark out so
clear where's good and where's the last place ya want to be
seen with a tiny little baby.

A BOY *and a* GIRL *suddenly appear in the light.*

BOY. How ya?

*All sounds stop. Just the normal sound of the city can be
heard.*

Long pause.

LITTLE LAMB (*to audience*). What can ya do but stop and
say . . . How yas?

BOY. Are ya goin ta give us money?

LITTLE LAMB (*to audience*). I'm trapped, yeah? My walkin
feet go dead quiet. I'm just waitin. (*Slight pause.*) S'like
I'm due a beaten for what I robbed on me da. I wiggle me
toes in me shoes and feel his money notes crinkle up. Two
hundred and fifty smackers in each shoe. An I stand there
waitin for what's next . . . just waitin . . . (*Whispers.*) Bang!

Loud noise/music as the BOY *and* GIRL *drag* LITTLE
LAMB *to the ground and kick the fuck out of her. The* GIRL
carries on punching LITTLE LAMB *in the face with the
bottom of* DOVE's *baby bottle which she takes from* DOVE,
as the BOY *grabs the pram and shakes it up and down
while screaming 'Baby baby baby baby baby baby . . . !'
Sound of* DOVE *screaming.*

Lights fade up on STEVE *sitting on the couch and weighing
the heroin and spooning little bits into small plastic bags.
He accidentally gets a tiny bit of heroin on his hand and
frantically wipes it off with his handkerchief.*

Fade up on LEP *on the bus. He speaks to the audience. His delivery is drowsy and very slow.*

LEP. Would you look at the fuckin head on Dublin out there, hey? Like some concrete caravan park. Is like a mongrel of a city – and all us on a great big summer holiday. We're full a life aren't we. All sorts of colours too all lookin up to the lovely blue sky. I fuckin love it up there. Like I'm lookin inta my lovely baby Dove's blue eyes. Lovely. I feel like one of those cuddly toys in one of those glass boxes . . . the steel hand hovering above me . . . wanting to toss me out the bus. But not me pal! I'm a slippery cunt the best of times and right now nothing can make me get off. Is just so lovely in here with yous! You're sort a like me brothers and sisters now ya know. I feel all close like I know you for ages. Don't like to use the word love but in your case I sorta have ta. I love ya. It's good to speak the mind, I like listening to it sometimes. (*He looks around and sees that there's no one on the bus.*) I feel alone now. Alone's okay though. But I feel like glass. A little glass man in a stone tumble drier that's what I'm feeling right now. Everythin feels cold. So I shut my eyes and try to find a safe place. It feels fucking lonelier in there pal. I want the bus to stop now. Maybe my sis can wrap me up in her beefy arm and make me feel new. I wish I was a chocolate eclair. She'd pop me right in. Watch Lep stretchin out inside my fat sister . . . swishin around in all that warm goo. (*Begins to cry.*)

Fade up on STEVE *putting on the Devil horns in his flat and walking through the moves he performed in the party the night before.*

LEP. I'm breakin up here I want ta be funny but I can't. Oh fuck. Come on Lep. Settle down pal. Just relax man. Try to think of a dream yeah. But I'm watchin the fuckin devil man. Messin with me. Me all babyish. When I see him I'm seeing my sweetheart's face. (*Begins to cry again.*) Oh Jesus fuckin Christ. Fuck sakes. Getting sad and scared now. Imagine me at me gaff. Lyin on the kitchen lino suckin in all that good off the silvery sheet. I can almost taste the fuckin thing. Chasin that little cheeky hot drop all around

and around. A lovely quick silver feelin. A lovely quick
silver feelin. Devil man is all gone . . . As Lep steps out into
the open blue sky with each little suck sweet stuff. (*Pause*.)
I need him.

We fade off LEP *who is lying on the bus floor and remain
on* STEVE *who has joined* AMANDA *on the couch reading
Hello! magazine.* STEVE *still wears the devil's horns. Fade
up the Humming Chorus from Puccini's Madame Butterfly.*
STEVE *is seated beside her listening to this beautiful music
with his eyes closed.* AMANDA *smokes and reads aloud
adopting a suitable posh voice. She is practising.*

AMANDA. Seeing Paul Young surrounded by his adoring
family in his strikingly large Art Deco home in North
London, it is difficult to imagine him as the hell-raising pop
idol who used to be mobbed in the streets. It looked as if
nothing could boost Paul and wife Stacey's, blissful
existence until the arrival of their second daughter, Layla.
(Main picture with Paul and piano.) (*Turns a page and
reads another article*.) Alexandra Bennet whose dream of
swimming for Britain in last year's Atlanta Olympics was
shattered when she was involved in a car crash, was told
only this month that she won't be able to make her expected
return to the pool under doctor's orders. The beautiful
brunette (19) broke both of her legs in a head-on car crash
while on her way to one of her regular training sessions.

Pause as AMANDA *takes it in. She laughs a bit. She then
folds her magazine closed on her knees. She goes to touch
STEVE's face but takes her hand away. After a long pause
as she stares around the flat. She sits on the coffee table
opposite* STEVE.

AMANDA. How now brown cow. How now brown cow. How
now brown cow.

STEVE. How a ya! Ya fuckin cow!!

The Humming Chorus comes to its natural finish.

Lights up on LITTLE LAMB *kneeling beside the pram.
Blood is pouring from the top of her head onto her face.*

She wipes it with her hand. Two GIRLS *approach her and look in the pram.*

GIRL 1. She's lovely isn't she?

LITTLE LAMB. Yeah.

GIRL 2. Ah look.

GIRL 1. It's a girl isn't it?

LITTLE LAMB. Yeah she is.

GIRL 2. Boys can't wear yellow can they?

GIRL 1. She got a scare did she?

LITTLE LAMB *nods her head.*

GIRL 2. Bet she's a survivor though.

GIRL 1. I'd love a baby of me own.

GIRL 2. Imagine all the nappies though. Do you get used to that?

LITTLE LAMB. Not really.

GIRL 1. My brother had yellow shite for two weeks.

GIRL 2. Fuckin hell!

GIRL 1. It's all right though. I mean that's natural.

LITTLE LAMB. Yeah.

GIRL 1. She's really lovely! Congratulations!

LITTLE LAMB. Thanks. (*Pause.*) I'm getting on a plane. I've got to get out of Dublin ya know.

GIRL 1 *nods her head.*

LITTLE LAMB. Is this the right road?

GIRL 1. Yeah it is.

LITTLE LAMB. Bye then.

GIRL 1. Yeah see ya.

Light comes up on STEVE *who is sitting on the couch.* AMANDA *is lying down with her head on his lap.*

AMANDA. Jesus Steve, ya smell beautiful. Like a man should ya know. Like you've been nature – formed. It's Fabergé, am I right Steve? Well it has to be really. Old Spice in the mornings, Fabergé dans le jour in the afternoon, French style. Sweetness. (*Long pause.*) How long do I have to lie here knickerless and gummin for it, Steve?!!

STEVE. Try shuttin the fuck up once in a blue moon, can't ya? Or can ya do that, love? Will ya do that for me, Amanda?

AMANDA. I need some affection.

STEVE. Have a wank!!

AMANDA. From you, ya bollix! From my very own man, Steve!!

STEVE. I don't want *it!* Is it not enough that I'm here for ya?!!

AMANDA. Ohhh pile it on pile it on pile it on!!

STEVE. Make me feel like second best and I'll break your fuckin face wide open! Like ya know I can, like ya know I will!

AMANDA. Let's give it a try again! Strip down, fool around! I know ya can, Steve! It'd be good and deep down I know ya want it, Steve! I can't go on waitin!! Is been fuckin ages!! I can't wait!

STEVE. Leave me and you'd die! Step outta this flat . . . they'd grab ya on that stair-well like they would me!! Batter ya with bats, burn ya alive as I'm watchin from the safety of our domestic bliss where my rules keep us ship-shape am I right!??! Am I right!!

AMANDA. Yes!

STEVE. Batter ya for killin their dirty junky little cunts of kids and you lyin screamin your tits off 'cause ya want a child of your own, when ya know I can't, ya know I won't do it!!

AMANDA. I don't want a kid anymore!! I want to fuck!!

STEVE. WON'T CAN'T DON'T!!! Give it a fuckin rest, Amanda!! (*Pointing to head.*) You're in here!! Mixin me up till all is mess, till a beatin is all that's left!! This is fuckin torture locked up in here with you actin' like that . . . always a beggin, always beggin!! Have a wank ya dosey cow! Ya don't want these angry hands wrapped around ya! Believe me, love!!

AMANDA. Love? Okay, love. (*Pause.*) I'll get ya in me dreams! Have a nap. I'll have ya when I'm asleep. Pretend.

STEVE. Look just close your eyes. I'll touch your hair till ya drop off, all right!

AMANDA. Yeah thanks.

AMANDA lies down with her head on STEVE 's lap. He pats her hair.

Sounds of bus fade in. LEP lies resting on FAT's lap. She looks out.

FAT. The slimey greasy bastard.

Fade up on LITTLE LAMB with DOVE. She spits on a piece of toilet paper and cleans her face of the blood.

Fade up on two teenagers. A BOY and a GIRL. The BOY stands opposite her shadow boxing. This continues for some time.

GIRL. Why don't ya just kiss me?

The BOY stops and looks around him.

BOY. Okay.

Lights up on STEVE and AMANDA. STEVE is on the couch and AMANDA is standing lighting a cigarette. The Flower Song by Lakme is playing once more. The sound of the bus's indicator is mixed with the piece of music and is then faded out. STEVE and AMANDA listen to the duet without giving expression to the very loud shouts of 'OUT OUT OUT!' 'outside' their flat. AMANDA reaches behind the cushion and takes up the cuddly teddy bear without STEVE noticing it.

Lakme plays low. AMANDA pulls away at a cigarette.

AMANDA (*to audience*). 'How the fuck can ya fancy a bloke who listens to that shite? Oper-ahs all about fat people tryin to get through constipation!' Ma and Gerard piss their sides as Little Lamb looks at me da like he was Benny Fuckin Hill, him lookin at her like she was the Virgin Fuckin Mary!!

STEVE. What time is it?

Live at Three's theme music is heard and continues underneath the below. Lakme has stopped. We see and hear Derek and Thelma introducing items etc.

AMANDA. That time. (*Back to audience.*) He shuts up! Is my time of the day! It's not that I like Live at Three . . . not that Derek and Thelma are high up on my birthday list or anythin . . . not likely . . . they're right down nexta Fred and Rosemary West ta tell yas the truth! It just keeps Steve quiet. Rest of the time he's as fidgity as a goldfish in a microwave!! Slap Derek and Thelma on and he's all numb and dead. Incredible really!! (*Pause.*) Ta pass the time I imagine Derek havin a ride with Thelma. There'd be little flower arrangements all dotted about!! Some ponce be bangin away on the old piano with an oul one warblin out some Irish fuckin ballad!! Derek and Thelma keepin time!! Derek's king size manky kax fallin down half mast down his chubby white legs. Thelma's teddy-bear dead eyes suddenly all a flicker as Derek reaches for the stars!! (*Laughs. Slight pause.*) I'd say Derek Davis reckons he's a great ride and Thelma Mansfield's as dry as a desert . . . or as me. Keeps me alive thinkin like that!! Stupid! But it colours me day most times. Today more than all day's. (*Pause.*) Once upon a long time ago he was mad inta doin it!! Toilets, parks, beaches . . . he once tried to reef me knickers down at midnight mass during Away in the Manger . . . 'There's always room in your Inn!!', he whispered inta me ear. But there's no touchin now. Just this grabbin and pushin. Like I'm a stranger. None of the old Steve all of a sudden. (*Pause.*) I'd see Little Lamb's baby Dove an imagine me own. Little red-raw arse on it and everythin! I'd lie it down on the bed . . . gurglin away and tryin ta find the word mammy or mama or ma. Hurts to know that inside you've got all the right ingredients. Steve got me a food processor when I wanted a feel. (*Pause.*) I want him to touch me now. I look at the same big fat hands that wrestled my little sister down last night. And here's me tryin ta place a tiny born baby in those hands. Wishin he'd take me now. Feel sick with these bad thoughts. He's made the word 'love' filth in my book. (*Long pause.*) Steve? Deep down I know you want to Steve. Baby.

He stares ahead ignoring her. Sounds of 'OUT! OUT! OUT!' from outside are fading up once more. AMANDA forces the teddy bear into his face. He grabs the teddy bear and rips it to pieces and forces it into her mouth while hitting her. Sounds fade up to loud. AMANDA gets up from the couch. STEVE sits crying into his hands. She calmly tidies up the mess. She then walks to the door and undoes each lock. Sounds suddenly stop.

Lights up on FAT *and* LEP *on the bus. Bus sounds. A boy gets on the bus with his new Discman. He sits on the seat and spits on the ground.* LEP *is collapsed in his seat.* FAT *is holding another chocolate éclair. She slowly begins to eat it. Meticulously she licks out the cream with a stiff tongue. With her teeth she scrapes off the chocolate. The sweetness of the chocolate hits a raw nerve in her teeth, she grimaces a bit. She dissects the éclair further by tearing it in two. She nibbles at one piece pulling it into her mouth with her teeth while rolling the other piece in her hands into a tight ball. Once finished the one in her mouth she quickly pops the other in. She then notices the audience.*

FAT. It's not like me to talk but I will! This bus is openin up my little brother Lep that's makin me feel sad. What a big ugly book his life is. An I wanna talk. I'm gonna tell yas everythin. I want ya to bring it home and tell someone else, an get that someone to tell someone else. Then the world might see a happy way out. (*Pause.*) Eat. Don't ever stop. Just eat and eat. Be the fattest. Be the ugliest, the most useless. Make yourself the lowest. From there things look better. Little small ugly things they get a beauty. People look beautiful. And *everything* is full of *wonder*. See I've been making myself nothing for nearly ten years. But I'm fillin days, starin into the stank grey and I'm findin little jewels. I'm findin little jewels that maybe one day you can see. (*Pause.*) What happened last night was really bad. The whole day's been full of his face. And I've been thinkin so hard about then. It all hurts. Things need putting straight. S'like I can't see the wonder anymore. I just see him. Him.

Loud noise/music as FAT *gets up. She stands above the boy with the Discman and calmly robs it off him.*

FAT *and* LEP *stand facing out as the music/noise continues. When it stops they burst through the door of* STEVE *and* AMANDA's *flat.*

STEVE. How did yous get in?

FAT. What are doors for? Haven't ya found out?

STEVE. What about *them?*

FAT. It's you they want.

LEP. Little cunts!

FAT (*handing* STEVE *the Discman*). We got ya this! He needs a deal!

STEVE. Can lepers live this long, Amanda? (*He laughs.*)

FAT. When's happy hour over?

AMANDA. Sit down, your almost family.

LEP. What is it about you that makes me feel all holy all of a sudden!?! I'd walk a million miles for none of your smiles! Ya smooth bastard! What I wouldn't give for five minutes in your shoes! Knobbin your wife an all, could I do that Steve, if I got my wish pal?! Imagine snugglin up in here! (*Smells* STEVE's *hand.*) That sex I smell?! Has ta be said it has ta be sex! Am I right!? You been waxin him or the couch, Amanda!?

AMANDA. Shut up Lep!!

LEP. Family was it? That's what you said, pretty?!!!

STEVE (*looking at the Discman*). What is this?

FAT. A kettle.

STEVE. It's Japanese, yeah?

LEP. It's a Discman, isn'it!? State a the art!! The rage, man!!
Cost ya a packet an all!

STEVE. Cheap shit!!

Slight pause.

LEP. What are ya bleedin sayin, Steve?!! That's money in the
hand!!

STEVE. Piece a crap!

Slight pause.

LEP. What are ya sayin? What's he fuckin sayin, Amanda!!
You been feedin him funny food or what!?!

STEVE. Ya got anythin' else?

LEP. Is this a joke, yeah?! Give us the fuckin score!!

STEVE. Got a T.V?

LEP. A what?

STEVE. Bring us a racehorse, Lep, then we're talkin!

LEP. A what? A fuckin horse!! Stop the fuckin messin!!
(*Laughs a bit.*)

STEVE. Call back tomorrow!

LEP. Jesus Christ, Steve!!

STEVE. I can't do it pal!!

LEP. What's he sayin, Fat?! What's all this bleedin chat about?
Stop all this bleedin chat and hand over, Steve!! I'm fuckin
dyin here!! Is all I got! I was workin me hole off ta get that
yoke!! Just take it or somethin!! Jesus Amanda, come on
please!! I'm beggin ya here, please!! COME FUCKIN ON!!
GIVE ME IT!

AMANDA. Just give him it!

STEVE. This is business!!

AMANDA. Save us some time!!

STEVE. What do we need with time?!! You busy or somethin!!

AMANDA. Don't know, am I?

STEVE. What ya mean by that?

AMANDA. Am I busy, Steve!?

STEVE. Shut the fuck up!

AMANDA. You shut the fuck up!

FAT. Give him the fuckin deal and shut the fuck up all a yas!! Think anyone's havin a good time? It's no joke!! That bloke's my little brother, so hand over can't ya?

STEVE. Since when can shite talk?

FAT. Well they never did break the mould with you!! I been talkin for years!! Since when do you listen?!!

STEVE. What was that?

FAT. Spastic man!!

STEVE. Sharp, aren't ya?

FAT. Cut your bleedin throat!!

    STEVE *tosses* LEP *some heroin in a tiny bag.* FAT *takes out an éclair and eats it.* LEP *begins the process of lighting up the Heroin and smoking it off the foil.*

STEVE. Any problems with this I'll make you pulp, all right!! (*Looks at* FAT.) Didn't ya get your tea, then? This all part of it, Fat? Don't you ever fuckin wash? Don't you ever get fed up with smellin rank and lookin like a knarlly old shite? Maybe you want to think of doin us all a big favour! The game's up ya big fat slag! Nothin's special here, puddin! Bottom line is you're a hippo and there's fuck all use for hippos about Dublin 'cept for the Zoo!! Now is this Dublin Zoo, Amanda?

AMANDA. Yes.

STEVE (*to* FAT). You make me sick!

FAT. You make my brother sick!! You just get on my fucking nerves!

STEVE. Clean up and fuck out!!!

FAT. A nice party, wasn't it?

STEVE. Was till you stank your way in!!

STEVE *puts on The Flower Duet on the stereo once more.*

FAT. You know what I'm talkin about! Last night!

STEVE. I'd rip your fuckin head off 'cept it only make ya prettier!!

FAT (*to* AMANDA). You make me so sad!! This whole flat smells of it!! Bein' cleanin all day, yeah?? Sprayin and scrubbin it all a lovely fresh smell!! But what's the point, Amanda?? What's the fuckin point when real filth's all about?!

AMANDA. Ya think I can't see that?!! See all of this shite for what it really is!!

STEVE. GET THE FUCK OUT!!

FAT. We're tryin!! We're tryin ta get out!! This is pain for us!! I just wanta ta come back!! See it again and say my little bit for what it's worth!! Leave with a clear head for what we all fuckin done last night!! This flat is spittin up all sorts of nasty pictures for me and Lep and outside's no better!! It's all hard!! A fuckin hard place with hate hate hate!! You make me want to puke, you piece of death, you fuckin thief!! We're tryin to fuckin get out of it!! Me and Lep are doin our best with it, YOU FUCKER!!!

LEP. This is good. (*Pause.*) Where's me baby! (*Pause.*) Little Lamb! (*Long pause.*) Us back, Steve! Steve, it's just like the party again! Class act that was, Steve!! Class! (*Long pause. To* FAT.) Take us home now, will ya?

Sounds of 'OUT OUT OUT' are fading up to very loud. FAT and LEP exit though the door. AMANDA follows leaving STEVE alone in the flat. Sounds suddenly stop.

Light fades up on LITTLE LAMB *and* DOVE. *Sounds of airport.*

LITTLE LAMB. All of a sudden life's a mad circus!! There's that amount of colour here you could sprinkle it all over a massive trifle and be eatin it for bleedin weeks!! Fuckin rapid, it is!! Deadly!! Hundreds of people settin out for hot spots!! 'Costa Del Fuckin Anywhere But Manky Stinkin Dublin', is a favourite destination!! Thousands of people headin off inta the sun!! All smilin and hoppin up and down like toddlers wantin a piss!! (*Laughs.*) I watch those arrivin back!! Like a bleedin morgue down there in Arrivals!! Worse!! But they're real tanned and sorta continental as they head for the Airport Pub ta mill back the pints!! Numbs the pain of comin back, I suppose!! Well I'm never comin back!! Never!! *Adios Dublin!!* Ya useless fat sweaty bum hole!! I'm fuckin out of here!! 'Whatever ya can give me!!' I said it ta the girl like it was natural! 'There's a cancellation to Majorca, Spain'. 'I'll pay in cash!!' Out with the money!! I think she could smell me feet off the notes, but fuck it, what do I care?! I'm too busy mappin out a new life ta worry about some snotty faced young one!! Ticket in me hand and I can see me on a beach!! The lovely sand and then the sea lappin up on it in the evenin with me as a waitress in a beach-bar servin up cocktails and just listenin ta the sound of Spain!! Me tanned, glowin and all natural! The warm sand squishin up through me toes! What's that funny warmness in your belly, Little Lamb?! That's me feelin happy!! Better get use to it love!! That feelin's stickin around for more than Summer!! I keep thinkin of all that I'm gonna do cause what I gotta do next is so hard and might seem nasty but it has ta be done!! (*Slight pause.*) I take me hands off the pram and leave!! I can sorta hear Dove beginnin ta whinge a bit and I want ta pick her up and give her a hug . . . kiss my man Lep with that very same hug goodbye . . . but I'm afraid!! Afraid I'll end up stayin here and never gettin out!! Watch me dream be sucked back inta Dublin! Afraid that I'll end up bringin her and things would be too hard for me!! Too hard for Dove!! Give her a chance, yeah?!! Just walk on!! Leave her for someone ta be a good mammy and daddy!! Might seem fuckin nasty but

I gotta be hard!! Have ta be!! Where does softness get me but another helpin of more pain!! I can still feel Steve. Taste his mouth in my mouth. (*Pause*.) Some fat security guard who looks like he hates his job snatches me ticket. (*Pause*.) All I love is gone. But in front I've got me with whatever I want. I spit up the taste of Steve and manky skinkin Dublin. I'm gettin the fuck out of here!

LITTLE LAMB *exits. Fade out sounds and lights off the pram alone on stage.*

Blackout.

The end.